Finding Your Soul

Workbook

By
Don Durrett

Copyright © 2011 Don Durrett
All Rights Reserved
(Third Edition November 2023)

No part of this book may be reproduced in any form or by any electronic or mechanical means including information storage and retrieval systems, without permission in writing from the author.

ISBN: 978-1-4276-5334-5

www.dondurrett.com

Books by Don Durrett

A Stranger from the Past

Finding Your Soul

Conversations With an Immortal

Spirit Club

Last of the Gnostics

The Gathering

Ascension Training

Team Creator

Your Soul Explained

The Path Forward

Get Healthy / Stay Healthy

America's Political Cold War

Post America: A New Constitution

The Demise of America

O man of honor, die before you die.

— Rumi

Die unto thyself.

— Jesus

I woke up and everything was so peaceful. The peace was there because there was no self.

— Eckhart Tolle

Become an empty vessel.

— various masters

Contents

Books by Don Durrett..iii
My Ten Favorite Spiritual Laws.................................ix
Introduction..xi

Chapter One
Finding Your Soul..1

Chapter Two
A Proactive Approach..3
   Chapter Two Exercise...6

Chapter Three
Know Your Self..7
   Chapter Three Exercise...11

Chapter Four
What is the Ego?..13
   Chapter Four Exercise..16

Chapter Five
Feeding the Ego...17
   Chapter Five Exercise...22

Chapter Six
Love and Trust...25
   Chapter Six Exercise...28

Chapter Seven
A Spiritual Path..29
   Chapter Seven Exercise..31

Chapter Eight
Morning Checklist..33
   Chapter Eight Exercise...39

Chapter Nine
Spiritual Practices to Create a New Humanity........41

Appendix
Sample Checklist..45

My Ten Favorite Spiritual Laws

1) Everything is vibrating energy, from the earth and rocks and trees, to the cells in our bodies. And all energy is conscious, interrelated, and interconnected.

2) The mind is the builder. As you sow, so you reap. Our thoughts and beliefs create our experiences.

3) The most important principles to live by are love, truth, and integrity.

4) Spiritual awareness is the highest achievement.

5) Like attracts like.

6) There is no such thing as chance or an accident. All is perfection.

7) Everything is playback, and everything has already occurred.

8) The truth shall set you free. What is the truth? Recognizing that you are one with God.

9) The meaning of life is the evolvement of the soul.

10) The soul is within and is the only way to the truth.

Introduction

The last chapter of my book, *Finding Your Soul*, evolved from my spiritual practices. I began with a single page of spiritual practices that I wanted to incorporate into my life. Then, each morning at breakfast, as I read my "morning checklist," as I called it, I would add to it. Over a period of a few years, it evolved and eventually grew into a PowerPoint presentation.

The next logical thing was to convert my presentation into a workbook, which is what you are about to read. The material is from my spiritual quest of getting closer to my soul and the result of what I have learned.

These are my ideas and concepts of how to find your soul. I am sure it is not for everyone, and that many of you will have your own ideas and concepts of how to achieve this objective.

As you read it, consider it a template that you can modify for your needs. In other words, take from it what you will and leave the rest.

* * * * *

There are going to be millions of people looking for spiritual answers as societal change overwhelms us. One area of inquiry is going to be the New Age movement and metaphysical concepts. This is inevitable because that is the future of spirituality. For this reason, I have been writing my books and this workbook. It is my hope that they can be of benefit to those looking for spiritual answers.

I decided to write a workbook so that people could use it to create a spiritual path. In many ways, it is a shortcut for something that took me years to achieve. In this book, I will provide exercises that will teach you how to pursue a spiritual path and get closer to your soul. If you do all of the exercises, not only will you find your soul, but your level of spiritual awareness will increase dramatically.

I wish you the best and hope that this book has a positive impact on your life.

Don Durrett
November 2023

Chapter One

Finding Your Soul

Finding your soul is a natural process. In fact, there is nothing to do, only to be. You do not have to proactively pursue religious or spiritual knowledge or pursue some form of salvation. The truth is that all you need to do is live your life as you see fit, and you will evolve. The reason why is that your soul and your ego are entwined. You can try to live completely from your ego, but your soul (higher self) will find a way to exert some influence.

This is why you don't have to look for your soul to find it. The fact is that **everyone has a spark of light that is expanding**. This spark of light is our soul, and it has an agenda of its own. Eventually our spark of light will expose the soul. This will happen without any effort on our part, although not necessarily in this lifetime.

Everyone is on their own journey and will pursue spirituality in their own time and manner. This is a long journey of many lifetimes. And everyone's journey has the same goal: finding our soul and understanding it. Quite often, we are not even aware that *is* our goal. In fact, most people have no clue that is their ultimate goal.

Everyone will eventually find their soul. This is guaranteed because of our spark of light that is constantly expanding. The soul does not regress (well, for 99.9% of us). It either stays stagnant or expands. The soul expands at a faster rate when you feed it. Conversely, when we feed the ego, we slow our rate of growth. However, there is no right way to find the soul. Eventually, we all find it.

One question I always get is, "**How will I know if I have found my soul?**" The answer is when you no longer feel alone. Meaning that you will feel a tangible connection with your soul, which will exist as a separate entity and as a part of your consciousness. Of course, this entity isn't separate, but it will feel that way. More importantly, it will feel real, and it will seem to be a powerful companion. Once you are aware of this companion, you will have found your soul.

I was once at a New Age conference, and it was mentioned that enlightenment is why we are here on this planet. We each have our own personal mission in this lifetime, which has the ultimate goal of enlightenment (although perhaps not in this lifetime). And that enlightenment is ultimately accomplished by discovering the soul. Moreover, this discovery is accomplished by clearing the mind of false beliefs and ideas, and getting closer and closer to the truth.

Perhaps the biggest secret of spirituality is that while the truth can set you free, the truth is not easily known. The starting point is to clear the mind from what is blocking you from the soul. Your mind has to metaphorically be rewired so that the truth is the driver. This requires spiritual practices. You have to become aware that it is your false beliefs that are blocking you from your soul. You can do this using a natural process (the slow way), or you can do it proactively (using the methods explained in this book).

Chapter Two

A Proactive Approach

While finding your soul is a natural process that everyone is already doing, **you can use a proactive approach to finding your soul more effectively.** This is for those who have a longing desire to search for a deeper meaning to life, and to understand who we really are. Those who search are often called seekers. For most seekers, at some point, there is an awakening.

This **awakening is about knowing that your soul exists**. It is not about faith. When you find your soul, you will know that you have found it. There is no 'maybe' or 'possibly.' You will know, and that process is about awakening.

However, to find your soul, **you have to do the work**. When you go on a spiritual quest to find answers that you yearn to understand, it takes effort and persistence. The purpose of this workbook is to give you insight into that work, and what it can require to have an awakening.

The starting point is to marginalize the ego. My personal experience on a multi-decade spiritual quest is that the ego has to be marginalized in order to expose the soul. Unless you marginalize the ego, the soul is submerged, and the ego takes center stage. One of them is going to run your life, and you have to choose which one.

Most of you know the definition of marginalize, but I will repeat it for those who are unsure. To marginalize is to reduce something in a proactive manner. For instance, to marginalize smoking in restaurants, we made it illegal. To marginalize your ego, you need to use proactive behaviors to reduce its influence.

A proactive approach to finding your soul is accomplished with a spiritual path. This requires a new lifestyle, a lifestyle of spirituality. This is not something that is periodic and must be done on a constant basis: minute by minute, second by second. You have to live your quest to find your soul.

Now we come to the hard part. The soul is pure and innocent, and that is all it knows, along with unconditional love. So, for you to have a relationship with your soul, that is how you have to become. You have to live the best version of you. You have to live with virtue and integrity.

Once you begin to live with virtue and integrity, you are ready to begin listening to your soul. You do this by keeping your mind quiet and remaining neutral. This is called the frequency of love. You accept everything that happens in your life as either a blessing or an opportunity. Instead of reacting to an event or situation, you remain neutral and then decide if it is a blessing or an opportunity.

This won't be easy at first, but you will get better over time. This is a spiritual practice. You are learning to be the best version of yourself, and you are learning to listen to your soul.

As you continue to keep your mind quiet, you will be opening a channel to your soul. And since you are now on the same wavelength as your soul, it is only a matter of time before your soul begins talking to you. The most

Chapter Two - A Proactive Approach

likely communication at first will be feelings, such as I should do that.

Over time, the communication will become clearer to the point where your soul will feel like a friend who is always with you.

The key to this beginning phase is recognizing that the ego is the chatter in your head and wants to get your attention. You will need to learn how to quiet that chatter, and to recognize the difference between the chattering ego and the very subtle, quiet soul.

Chapter Two Exercise

- ☑ Begin a journal, and every morning, write down what you did the previous day with regard to a lack of integrity or a lack of virtue.

- ☑ If you have any bad habits, write them down and what you need to remove them.

- ☑ Begin paying attention to your thoughts. When thoughts come up, immediately go back to the present moment (go back to the silence). At first, this will seem impossible, but over time, with persistence, you will learn to keep your mind quiet.

- ☑ Begin to recognize that the chattering mind only wants to do one thing: think about the past or the future. The past is irrelevant, and the future hasn't happened yet. Only focus on what you need to do in the present moment.

- ☑ Begin to recognize that the soul only exists in the present moment, and try to live there as much as you can.

Chapter Three

Know Your Self

Knowing your personality traits is extremely useful for finding your soul. Why? Because your ego knows your traits, and you need to be armed with the same information. The ego is your nemesis and does not want you to find your soul. This is something you will discover very quickly once you begin to quiet your chattering mind. The ego will push your buttons in order to control you. The ego will do everything it can to subvert your desire to have a relationship with your soul.

The ego is not your friend and does not care about your well-being. In fact, the bigger the mess of your life, the more control the ego has. Your mission is to find your soul, and the ego's mission is to subvert that outcome.

So, if you are going to do a psychological battle with the ego, then you need to level the playing field by understanding the buttons the ego plans to push. Those buttons are all related to your personality weaknesses.

You have to learn about your ego traits and your goals for this lifetime. Basically, you have to figure out what you're here to do, and what mask you are wearing to accomplish this goal.

Astrology. The natal chart: Astrology has been around for thousands of years, and it is very accurate. This is a tool the Creator has given us to do battle with the ego, to make this challenging life a bit more fair. I have done natal charts for more than a hundred friends and relatives, and they are usually very accurate. A natal chart is usually 20 to 30 pages if it is done with computer software. It includes an enormous amount of information and will help you to understand your personality traits.

For instance, my sun sign is Pisces. This makes me sensitive, intuitive, creative, soft, imaginative, and dreamy. I have all of those traits. My rising sign is Cancer. This makes me a double water sign. This makes me highly sensitive and highly emotional, which is an easy trigger for my ego to attack. If someone says something mean to me, it can hurt more than a physical blow, and stay with me for days, months, even years. Cancer is ruled by the moon and that makes me moody, and my emotions go up and down like a yo-yo. The ego knows this. My moon is in Sagittarius. This is the sign of philosophy, and I am a spiritual philosopher. It is also a fire sign, which gives me passion and energy. However, it also gives me a temper which I have to control. Again, another button for my ego.

Learn all of the sun signs. This will help you to understand your moon sign and rising sign. Those three will tell you a lot about your ego.

Numerology. My two favorite books on this subject are *The Life You Were Born to Live* by Dan Millman, and *Glynis Has Your Number* by Glynis McCants. Both of these books are excellent tools for understanding your ego. I cannot emphasize enough how valuable they are. Dan Millman's book is stunningly accurate. I am a 28/10. Which is derived from my birth day 3/18/1960, or 3 + 1 + 8 + 1 + 9 + 6 = 28. 2 + 8 = 10. 1 + 0 = 1. Thus, my lifepath is 28/10 or 1. In Dan's book, I am a 28/10. In Glynis book,

I am a 1 lifepath. 1's are initiators and self-starters. I start something, I usually finish it. I am always working on a project or thinking of my next project. That is typical for 1 energy.

In Millman's book, he actually explains the lessons we came to accomplish. It's almost as if the Creator wanted to share information with us to make our lives easier. With this information, we know what the ego knows about us. Once we know, the ego loses some of the buttons it wants to push.

The Science of the Cards. My two favorite books on this subject are *Love Cards* by Robert Camp and *Cards of Destiny* by Sharon Jeffers. I thought I knew myself, and then a friend of mine told me I was a 5 of diamonds. I bought Robert Camp's book and read about the 5 of diamonds. I was amazed. Basically, it said that I am a restless seeker of truth and that I was likely single because of my restlessness and desire for freedom. It was an eye-opener and spot-on accurate. One more tool the Creator has given us to wage war with the ego and find the soul.

How did this book know me so well? It was science. My birthday reflects the mask that I had chosen in this lifetime.

Everyone should know their card and what it represents. This system is incredibly accurate and gives excellent insight into our personality.

The Michael Teachings. My favorite book on this subject is *Messages from Michael* by Chelsea Quinn Yarbro. The Michael Teachings are about the reincarnation cycle. Here you learn about the goals of the soul. You can read the book and guess at your soul level and role. I guessed old soul and priest. Then I had a reading and found out that I was a 5th-level old soul, priest, with a sub role of scholar. That fits me perfectly and resonated with my heart. This knowledge got me closer to understanding my life goal, which is to help humanity raise its vibration.

You may think that all of these methods are a bunch of baloney and are fake. You won't feel that way once you use them to figure out your personality traits. Instead, you will wonder why they aren't more popular.

Spiritual & Psychic Readings: tarot, clairvoyants, mediums, hypnotic regressions, life between life regressions. Spiritual readings are where you learn more about both your ego traits and your soul's goal for this lifetime. I have had about two dozen readings, and they have all led me to the understanding that I am an ancient spiritual philosopher who is here to help with the coming spiritual transformation of humanity. Your readings will likely continue until you are very clear on your ego traits and life goals. After that, they are no longer needed. After that, the ego no longer has an edge in the battle.

Chapter Three Exercise

- ☑ Have your natal horoscope done. The easiest way is to purchase it on the Internet, although a professional astrologer is the best way. I did both.

- ☑ Purchase or borrow *The Life You Were Born to Live* by Dan Millman and read about your lifepath and life goals. The accuracy of this information is profound.

- ☑ Use the Internet to find out what card (Science of the Cards) you are and read the description.

- ☑ Use the Internet and read about the Michael Teachings. Try to figure out if you are a mature soul or an old soul, and what role you are using in this lifetime.

- ☑ Have a spiritual reading of some type. I would recommend a one-hour reading from a psychic medium with good reviews. See if you can get an insight as to why you are here.

Chapter Four

What is the Ego?

The ego is our temporary personality. It is our mask. It is our role for this lifetime. It is the illusion we have chosen to use for the pursuit of finding our soul. Most people like their ego personality and perceive it to be who they truly are. The very thought of their ego being an illusion is unsettling. That alone prevents most people from pursuing a spiritual path.

The ego is not your true self. As I just said, it is an illusion. When you leave this lifetime, you will not take your ego with you. The hidden side of you, the true you, that is what you will take with you, along with all of your experiences.

The ego is not your soul. The ego was created for this one lifetime. The soul is permanent and is a combination of one's multiple life experiences.

The ego is hiding your soul. The ego and the soul are entwined but are separate. Until the soul is exposed by marginalizing the ego, the soul is submerged and hidden. Depending on our level of spiritual awareness, the soul will try to get our attention. However, anyone can try to find their soul. Anyone can be proactive.

The ego is our chattering mind. When I began my spiritual quest, I had no idea that my thoughts were my ego. The soul is primarily in the background being silent. It communicates to us by whispering and through feelings. It is the tiny voice within.

Temptation, frustration, fear, anger, and worry: these thoughts and feelings all originate in the ego. Our thoughts are literally our ego keeping us away from our soul. In fact, it is our thoughts that keep us blocked from our soul. Our ego does not care about our well-being. It is only concerned with its own existence.

The ego can never be satisfied. The ego is like an addiction. It is always waiting for an opportunity to gain control. If you think you can have an active mind, constantly thinking about the past and future, and at the same time be on a spirit quest, you are mistaken. The ego, in that situation, will be in charge. It will be the soul that is marginalized.

The present moment is where the soul exists, in the silence. The first twenty minutes after you wake up is a good time to do a self-check and see if you are living in the present moment. Most likely, you will be living in your chattering mind.

The ego and the soul are separate but appear to be entwined in your consciousness. It is important that you learn how to separate the ego and the soul. You do this by marginalizing the ego and feeding the soul. To expose the ego, ask these questions:

1) Is this the voice of the ego?

On the next few pages, I will show you the voice of the ego.

2) Is this for the higher good?

Chapter Four - What is the Ego?

The ego does not aspire to help humanity or help you. You can use this understanding to further marginalize the ego and to live for a higher purpose. If you recognize that your behavior is not for the higher good, you can instantly know that it is of the ego. And anything of the ego is taking you away from the soul.

3) Are you outside of your mind?

Within this workbook, I define the mind as your brain. The ego is in your head, and the soul is in your heart. The soul exists as part of our consciousness outside of the mind. Thus, you have to be out of your mind to find your soul.

When someone has an NDE (near-death experience) and leaves their body, they are surprised that they can think, remember, see, and hear without a body. This is from the soul consciousness.

Let me show you one way to step outside your ego. Become conscious of feeling your hands until you can feel them tingle. Notice that when you are feeling your hands, your mind goes silent. Why does this happen? The soul is taking over. You have just found your soul in the silence. You just opened the channel to the soul. Now, you have to learn how to keep it open. That's the hard part.

You have to learn how to have one foot in this world and one foot out. Spiritually aware people generally always have one foot in this world and one foot in the spirit realms connected to their soul. You can do this, too, with practice.

Chapter Four Exercise

- ☑ Each morning, write down instances yesterday where you experienced temptation, frustration, fear, anger, and worry. These thoughts all came from the ego and the chattering mind. As you expose the ego, you can marginalize it by remaining neutral and recognizing that all you get in life are blessings or opportunities.

- ☑ Recognize that the soul only knows unlimitedness, positive thoughts, joy, aliveness, unconditional love, success, and expansion. Each day become more aligned with this energy. The more aligned you become, the easier it is for the soul to give you guidance and direction.

- ☑ Create a stack of business cards with affirmations (use the list in the back of this book). Read these cards in the car at stop signs, or before you go to bed.

Chapter Five

Feeding the Ego

To find the soul and consistently interact with it, we have to live a lifestyle of integrity and virtue. Otherwise, the ego will submerge the soul and constantly feed itself. The following list is what most people commonly use to feed their egos. By studying these behaviors, you can marginalize them and keep them out of your life.

While that may not be possible to achieve simply by reading this list, you can slowly and steadily remove them from your life by pursuing a spiritual path.

Envy: I define this as **wanting something that someone else has because of jealousy.** Envy and greed are closely related. For instance, having a nice house, but wanting a nicer one because other people have them. Wanting more is a sign of envy. Instead of wanting more, we should accept what we have as what we need. This does not mean we shouldn't follow our passion, and where our heart wants to lead us.

Gluttony: Having too much of something that you don't need. The key here is knowing when to stop, and knowing when enough is enough. The ego tempts us that more is better when it often is not. Food and TV are good examples. Alcohol is another. Living simply and in moderation is the solution. This allows you the ability to limit gluttony.

Greed: Wanting more of something that you don't need. Envy and gluttony are related to greed. Normally, greedy people are also envious and gluttonous. They don't know when to say when. Or when they have had enough. Greed is a very selfish desire. Wall Street, the movie, has a scene where Darian, Bud's girlfriend, played by Daryl Hanna, is getting out of the ocean, and she looks up at Gordon Gecko's opulent beach house. She says to Bud, "If I could have this, it would almost be enough." That's the problem with greed, there is never enough.

Lust: Wanting some form of mental stimulation. This is the ego at its strongest. Lust can include just about anything that is hedonistic. The lust for sex, drugs, alcohol, nicotine, porn, junk food, and even sports, can be overwhelming. Al Pacino, as the 'devil' in the movie *The Devil's Advocate*, states that his favorite sin is vanity, which is essentially pride. But the ego's favorite sin is Lust. Lust can cause a myriad of problems, or even destroy our lives. The ego loves problems, no matter how dire. The lower we fall, the stronger the ego becomes.

Pride: Identifying with your ego. This is the last form of feeding the ego to overcome. The ego is the source of all pride. This is something you will learn if you attempt to marginalize the ego. All forms of feeding the ego are related to pride. In fact, pride is the most difficult belief to transform because pride is our individualness, which we don't want to give up. And the ego will try to convince us that our ego-identity is real and we shouldn't give it up.

Sloth: This is essentially laziness. We honor God/Creator with self discipline and responsibility. Conversely, we dishonor God/Creator and Self when we lack discipline and responsibility. This is another way to say that God/Creator cares about how we live our lives.

God/Creator has infinite patience and allows for all stages of growth, but ultimately God/Creator wants us to be highly responsible souls.

Wrath: This is what I like to call pride on steroids. Wrath is the telltale sign that the ego is in charge. If you get upset, that is your way of telling God that you are not content or grateful. You are saying, "God, I am not happy with the life you have given me. I do not love you, God. I am mad at you."

Old souls tend to be loving and gentle. That is how you can tell if they are old souls. You become gentle when you begin to recognize that you're an eternal being who is not only loved by God, but is literally one with God, and one with humanity. When you become close to enlightenment, you begin to recognize that by getting upset or angry at another, you are identifying with your ego.

If you have one foot in this world, and one foot in spirit, you can stand back from that anger and release it. The anger can start to rise, and you can nip it quite easily if you have that one foot in spirit. Moreover, if you can identify the ego, you can see that *that* is not you. Not the *real* you.

Ungrateful: This shows itself by lacking contentment and being unhappy. How can *not* being happy feed the ego? Because this is an unnatural state, created by negative emotions which come from the ego. If we are eternal souls who have been given the gift of life, and the gift of an opportunity to become as enlightened like Jesus or Buddha, then we should be grateful. As stated before, the only two things we get in life are blessings and opportunities. Everything else is an illusion.

Selfishness: This is caring more about yourself than humanity. This is where society has driven us. During my IT career, one company pushed me to be a high achiever, which was rewarded. They thought this was good business. But, in actuality, it instilled a sense of individuality and selfishness. There is a fine line between living for oneself and living for others. Try not to cross it because you will be feeding your ego.

Eventually, we come to learn that life is about service to humanity and not about self-service to one's self-interest. Corporations do not care about humanity. They care about the bottom line. They care about their self-interest. Selfishness is ingrained into us when we enter school and are given grades and forced to compete against one another. This mentality is carried forward into the business world. What no one recognizes is that, by being selfish, we are feeding our egos and not feeding our souls.

Arrogance: Feeling superior to others, dishonesty, being mean or willful. Arrogance feeds the ego, and these behaviors are always linked to pride. When we identify with the ego, this is pride. And when we go counter to our true self, it is the appearance of the ego. When these arrogant behaviors arise, they are nothing more than the ego hiding the soul. They are lessons that eventually expose the ego for what it truly is, a mask that only cares about its survival. Do we serve humanity or self? This is the question we eventually come to ask, although perhaps not in this lifetime.

Past/Future (Chattering Mind): This is where the ego lives. We feed our egos constantly with our chattering mind. For most people, this is an ongoing process that never ceases. For an aware soul, it is something that is controlled to a large extent. They consciously keep their mind quiet.

Fear: Lacking trust in God/Creator's eternal grace. After lust, fear is the ego's favorite weapon to push our buttons. Fear is created in our mind by our ego. It is only an idea. You don't have to be afraid. You choose to be afraid. With trust in our eternal destiny, there is no reason to fear. In fact, the truth and fear cannot coexist. If you can truly see that this world is an illusion and the soul is indestructible and cannot be damaged, then trust is possible. The ego uses fear to keep us trapped in the illusion of life. This will become apparent if you attempt to marginalize the ego.

Chapter Five Exercise

For the following list, try to remember specific instances when you used them to feed your ego. This is going to be informative and should create an epiphany or two on how your ego has controlled you in the past or is still controlling you. Once you are done, review the list several times with the objective of not repeating these instances.

You can't become innocent and pure overnight. That takes spiritual practice. But what you can do is strive to become the best version of yourself, and in better alignment with your higher self. Recognize that your higher self is innocent and pure, and that is the *real* you. The false you is the ego.

- ☑ Envy

- ☑ Gluttony

- ☑ Greed

- ☑ Lust

- ☑ Pride

- ☑ Sloth

- ☑ Wrath

Chapter Five - Feeding the Ego

☑ Ungrateful

☑ Selfishness

☑ Arrogance

☑ Chattering Mind

☑ Fear

Chapter Six

Love and Trust

Love yourself. This is why it is important to marginalize your ego. The ego will constantly make it difficult for you to love yourself. The reason for this is that if you truly love yourself, you will live a pure lifestyle. And the ego does not want to live a pure lifestyle. The ego wants to wallow in the seven deadly sins and feed itself.

Love others. Everyone is on a spiritual path. Respect and have compassion for others. Not because you agree with their choices, but in spite of them. This is where sensitivity and judgment come into play. Do not be sensitive to other's behavior that you disapprove of. Instead, recognize that everyone is on a spiritual path and their egos are most likely in charge. Have compassion for their lack of spiritual awareness. Be compassionate of the plight of others, even if it is uncomfortable for you to do so. The recommendation to not judge others is true wisdom.

Love God/Creator with honor and respect. Be true to yourself, and you will be true to God/Creator. Thus, live with integrity and be your authentic self. This can only be achieved by marginalizing the ego and feeding the soul.

Trust that your life was pre-planned and that you came with an objective to learn something. Before we incarnate, we carefully select a life that can teach us the lessons we need to learn. This selection is done through a planning process that analyzes future lifetimes. It is a highly complex process where many souls plan and incarnate together. The reason it comes off so smoothly is that everything has already happened. Life, in many ways, is simply playback or rewind. All events have already happened and are the imagination of God/Creator.

Trust that life is divinely ordered. This is why there are no accidents. Life is perfect, and God/Creator is running the show. We can think we have free will, but God/Creator is making sure that life is going according to plan. We do have a degree of free choice and can choose how we are going to live our day. But on most days when we wake up, our day has already been determined. Not because God/Creator is going to dictate what we choose, but because our beliefs are known to God/Creator, who can anticipate what we will choose. You see, it is our beliefs that dictate our behaviors. And it is our collective beliefs that dictate society's behavior.

Trust that nothing can happen to you that is not supposed to happen. This goes back to my previous answer. Our beliefs create our reality, and we create everything that happens in our life. Not one thing can happen that was not created by our beliefs. This seems impossible, but it is so. This is why we eventually come to learn over many lifetimes that the ego is causing all of our dysfunction and disharmony. At some point, we come to learn that we can either feed the ego or feed the soul.

The ego is so good at camouflaging its motives, that many of you will not even believe my statements about trust. The ego is a master of evoking doubt. After all, it is the ego's existence that is at stake. For, once you come to understand the ego and stop feeding it, it fades into the background. The ego will do everything it can to remain relevant.

Chapter Six Exercise

Write down what these concepts mean to you. Name some specific instances where you successfully used each of them. Review your answers in one year and see how much you have changed your beliefs.

- ☑ Love Yourself.

- ☑ Love Others.

- ☑ Love God.

- ☑ Trust that your life was pre-planned.

- ☑ Trust that life is divinely ordered.

- ☑ Trust that nothing can happen to you that is not supposed to happen.

Chapter Seven

A Spiritual Path

We are here to grow and develop mastery over the ego. It may not appear that way, but that is the meaning of life. It is all about achieving spiritual enlightenment.

Everyone's soul is vibrating at a particular frequency. This frequency equates to our spiritual development. When we leave our body, we will return to a place that is compatible with our frequency. We will then make plans on how to increase that frequency, i.e. raise our vibration, using specific experiences.

We use our life experiences to expand our spiritual awareness. That is why we are here. This life is not a vacation, although the ego tries to convince us that it is. The development of the soul is not a frivolous pursuit, although we can try to enjoy the ride. Still, it is not all fun and games.

Our spiritual path (if we choose to pursue one) is accomplished in two parts. Part one is learning how to not feed the ego, which is the most difficult. The second part is learning how to have a relationship with the soul. This is done by feeding the soul using prayer, keeping the mind quiet, keeping the channel to the soul open, meditating, reading spiritual material, going to seminars, doing yoga, et cetera. However, unless the ego is marginalized, your spiritual path will be impeded by your ego.

Note that by not feeding the ego, we automatically feed the soul. Simply by ignoring the ego, we open a communication channel to our soul for guidance. Moreover, by focusing on our life's goal, we feed the soul. This is part two of your spiritual path. Find out what you need to do in this lifetime, and then do it. Follow your heart (your passion) and go where you are led.

Every morning is a new day, a new opportunity to become more aligned with the soul. Live one day at a time, not feeding the ego. If you fail one day, then get up and start over. Always start a new day fresh. Don't carry over any baggage from yesterday, although that is easier said than done. Have you ever noticed while on a vacation that you felt fresh without any worries? You can do that every day. You don't have to bring your baggage into each new day. Our baggage is our ego forcing us to look back or look forward.

The ego is a worthy adversary and is quite strong. I personally read my morning checklist every day to make sure I do not give the ego an opening. If you focus on only aligning with the soul, then the ego is marginalized. You have to do this on a daily basis as part of your spiritual path, or else the ego will find an opening and push your buttons.

Chapter Seven Exercise

Answer each of these questions. Review them in a year

- ☑ Describe the methods you are using to develop mastery over your ego.

- ☑ Look at your negative behavior patterns. How are you feeding your ego?

- ☑ When you woke up this morning, what baggage did you bring with you from yesterday?

- ☑ How are you aligning with your soul?

- ☑ What is your life's goal? Why did you incarnate? If you don't know the answer, then find out using a psychic medium.

Chapter Eight

Morning Checklist

Here are some ideas to use to create your morning checklist. When I started mine, it constantly grew in size. Every morning, I would write down more ideas. It has evolved over the years. Today, it is down to ten items.

1) **Live pure.**
   - Don't feed the ego.
2) **Live present without a chattering mind.**
   - It is nearly impossible to never have a chattering mind. However, you can reduce its influence with proactive steps, such as paying attention to your thoughts. .
3) **Feed your soul.**
   - Do what brings you joy. Do what you love. Say what you love.
4) **Be content and accept your life.**
   - This is a tough one. We often want more. We compare our lives to those of others and are not satisfied. This is an ego trap. Recognize that your life is perfect and that all you get are blessings and opportunities.

5) **Be grateful and honor God/Creator.**
   - Gratefulness is one of the most powerful thoughts you can have. So, not only be grateful every day but try to remain in a constant state of gratitude.
6) **Live simply and try to simplify your life.**
   - There is a reason monks have few possessions. Your excess stuff will become a trigger the ego will use. The less possessions you own, the more harmony you will have, and the less to worry about.
7) **Live humbly and acknowledge that we are all equals.**
   - Being humble is the opposite of being arrogant. Humility is a trait of the soul, which is what we are trying to get closer to. Not only are we all equal, but we are, in fact, all sharing the same consciousness. This makes us all one family.
8) **Stay healthy by eating right and exercising.**
   - Good health and spirituality go hand in hand. Why? Because good health is one less obstacle we have to overcome to get closer to our soul. I became a vegetarian in 2004, and it was one of the smartest things I have done in this lifetime.
9) **Be enthusiastic and have passion for life.**
   - Follow your passion. That will lead you where you need to go. Follow your heart. It is always true.

10) **Live with one foot in this world and one foot in the spirit world.**
    - You do this by keeping the communication channel open with your soul at all times. Don't let your soul get too far out of your awareness, which can occur if you are not actively monitoring your thoughts.
11) **Stay on the path by living one day at a time.**
    - Keep a close eye on the ego and your life's goal. Monitor your progress every morning. Consider each day a restart, and path forward. Thus, the past no longer matters. It's just water under the bridge.
12) **Acknowledge the perfection of life.**
    - Recognize that everything has already happened and that it all comes from the imagination of God/Creator. Your life is perfect and giving you exactly what you need. You wouldn't be here if that wasn't true.
13) **Be compassionate with yourself and others.**
    - If you recognize the perfection of life, then it is much easier to be compassionate with yourself and others. Life is simply a series of lessons that are used for the growth of the soul.
14) **Take life lightly.**
    - Life is a gift. Life is an experience. I like to think of this lifetime as a blip of experience. It is just one lifetime. So, don't take it too

seriously. Everyone gets as many chances as they need to get it right.

15) **Let life come to you.**
    - Ride the energy. Follow your heart. Stay in the flow, following your intuition. Sometimes it can appear that nothing is happening in your life. However, in the background there is movement and change on the horizon. Be patient and wait for signs and cues from your soul to tell you what to do. And when they come, don't deny them. If the energy says to go this way, then ride it. Pay attention to your feelings! They are true.

16) **Don't make choices that impact your life negatively.**
    - This includes anything that feeds the ego. If you read this every morning, when you make a choice that impacts your life negatively, it will be apparent. You can then take steps to prevent this from happening again. Often a trigger will cause us to feed the ego. If you attempt to marginalize the ego, you will learn your triggers and the choices that you want to curtail. Your life will begin to change for the better, and your bad habits will wither away.

17) **Every day, try to have more trust in your soul and less fear.**
    - We either go to trust or go to fear. We all have an element of fear in our lives. With spirituality, you can reduce that fear with

trust. Who are we trusting? God/Creator, but also our soul, which is giving us direction. The soul is powerful and more aware of our needs than we are. In many respects, we are blind, and the soul is our eyes showing us where to go.

18) **Be gentle and compassionate. Be more like your true self.**

    - Be true to yourself and true to God/Creator. Initially, this is all about respect. We need to respect our true selves, humanity, and God/Creator. The more respect we have, the gentler we will be, and the less arrogant. Happiness (soul-driven) and fear (ego-driven) are choices. Before I became awakened, I had no idea that these were choices. I thought that happiness was something that was obtained, and that fear was natural. In fact, happiness is a frequency, and fear is created by the mind. Both are choices.

19) **Try to have less attachment to this world and more attachment to your soul.**

    - Why? Because this world is illusion and temporary. Recognize what is temporary versus what is permanent. It is the soul that is permanent and what you should try to become more attached to. The ego convinces us that the world is real, but it is not. The ego tricks us into placing our attention on it and ignoring the soul. When we consider putting more focus on the soul, the ego uses doubt to pull us back in. It takes considerable effort (spiritual practice) to focus on the soul and not the ego.

20) **Fear and temptations poison the mind.**
    - I read this in a book that channeled Mary Magdalene. I agree with her. I think they do poison the mind. How do we not have fear or temptations? We do spiritual practice. We might not completely eliminate them, but we will make progress.
    - When striving to eliminate temptations (addictions), you will have the greatest success if you focus on a positive behavior to replace what you want to eliminate. Make that positive behavior part of your daily checklist to keep it foremost in your mind. For instance:
        - Love for self, others, and God.
        - Recognition/awareness of what is important: love, truth, joy.
        - A personal mantra: We are one, be kind, be gentle.

Chapter Eight Exercise

☑ Create your own morning checklist of daily reminders. Try to list them in the affirmative wherever possible. For example: Live pure and love others.

☑ List behaviors that you want to avoid, such as addictions or deadly sins, until these behaviors have been overcome.

☑ List positive things you can do to replace negative behaviors or patterns, as this will help you to form better habits.

☑ Read your list every morning with your breakfast for 3-5 minutes. If it helps, read it again before bedtime.

As you read your list, make changes and modify it to fit your needs. I found that I generally made a minor change every day for the first six months. It felt like my soul was telling me what to add or modify.

Chapter Nine

Spiritual Practices to Create a New Humanity

1) **Selfless / Egoless.**
   - This is the new normal. Instead of being aggressive and striving to be number one, it is time to take it down a notch. It is time to feel at one with humanity and strive to get along with others.
2) **Compassionate / Caring**
   - The modern world has created an insensitive populace, where everyone is competing against each other. In the new humanity, we are going to create compassion and caring for all of humanity.
3) **Gentle / Loving Kindness.**
   - Many people are kind and gentle. In the near future, it will be nearly everyone. Why? Because there will be a new sense of connectedness and empathy. There will be a feeling of oneness.

4) **Fearless / Trusting.**
   - This will be one of the biggest changes for humanity. Currently, most people live in fear. As humanity becomes more spiritually aware, trust will become the norm.
5) **Purity / Humble.**
   - When you know that everyone is your equal, that makes you humble. And when you recognize that humility, living by purity becomes the natural way to live.
6) **Simple / Content.**
   - This means living simply and without extravagance. In the near future, living simply will be considered a virtue. Those who live simply will be the most content.
7) **Grateful / Honoring.**
   - People will be soft and gentle and quick to smile. This will be the result of their gratitude for the gift of life from our creator. People will honor God/Creator by acknowledging our heritage. Nature will be respected to a much higher degree than today.
8) **Courageous / Determined.**
   - Most people will be determined to build a better world. And they will be courageous enough to do whatever it takes to succeed. These human traits will be much more common than those existing today.

Chapter Nine - Spiritual Practices to Create a New Humanity

9) **Spirit Led / Heart Led.**
   - People will begin to lead themselves by their spirit. This is the biggest change coming for humanity. We will no longer need as many leaders to tell us what to do. We will know how to lead ourselves.

10) **Helpful / Generous.**
    - Soon, people will begin to feel an affinity with one another. Everyone will feel like family, the human family. As this change takes hold, the degree of generosity that manifests will be astounding, compared to what exists today.

APPENDIX

Sample Checklist

At the top, write down what you want to work on. Include the reasons why you want to change this behavior.

1) God IS; I AM; We ARE.

2) Are you serving humanity or self? Fork in the road choice: self or God?

3) Are you helping the cause (adding light), or are you hurting the cause (adding darkness)?

4) Observe your thoughts. Keep your mind quiet.

5) Purity of thought, walking the talk (becoming innocent).

6) Love of self and love of humanity (acknowledge your eternalness and life's oneness).

7) Lust/temptations. Is lust natural? Is anger natural? Or tests of the ego?

8) Recognize what is important: conscious living and soul growth.

9) Live simply and humbly.

10) Personal Mantra: we are one, so be kind and loving.

11) Do not raise your voice or get upset. Stay calm and gentle.

12) Stay healthy: eat right and exercise. Take care of the body.

13) Nothing to do; only to be. Become nothing. Then you have no baggage.

14) Every day have more trust and less fear.

15) Life is replay and fear is an idea.

16) Nothing can happen that is not perfect.

17) Our experiences are needed lessons. We create it all.

18) Envy (vanity), Gluttony (diet), Greed (materialism), Lust (pleasure), Pride (selfishness), Sloth (laziness), wrath (anger).

19) I do not want to be that selfish, angry, prideful person anymore.

20) I want to be a loving, kind, grateful person, who knows what is important.

This is a sample list for when you begin your spiritual practice. It will change significantly after a few years. Mine is nothing like this anymore.

www.ingramcontent.com/pod-product-compliance
Lightning Source LLC
Chambersburg PA
CBHW072113290426
44110CB00014B/1897